Pseudocode:

Functions/View

Methods:

Output:

Layout Design:

Notes

Notes

Pseudocode:	Functions/Views:
	Methods:

Output:

Layout Design:

Notes

Notes

Pseudocode:	Functions/Views:
	Methods:

Output:

Layout Design:

Notes

Notes

Pseudocode:	Functions/Views:
	Methods:

Output:

Layout Design:

Notes

Notes

Pseudocode:	Functions/Views:
	Methods:
Output:	

Layout Design:

Notes

Notes

Pseudocode:	Functions/Views:
	Methods:
Output:	

Layout Design:

Notes

Notes

Pseudocode:	Functions/Views:
	Methods:
Output:	

Layout Design:

Notes

Notes

Pseudocode:	Functions/Views:
	Methods:

Output:

Layout Design:

Notes

Notes

Pseudocode:	Functions/Views:
	Methods:

Output:

Layout Design:

Notes

Notes

Pseudocode:	Functions/Views:
	Methods:
Output:	

Layout Design:

Notes

Notes

Pseudocode:	Functions/Views:
	Methods:

Output:

Layout Design:

Notes

Notes

Pseudocode:	Functions/Views:
	Methods:

Output:

Layout Design:

Notes

Notes

Pseudocode:	Functions/Views:
	Methods:

Output:

Layout Design:

Notes

Notes

Pseudocode:	Functions/Views:
	Methods:

Output:

Layout Design:

Notes

Notes

Pseudocode:	Functions/Views:
	Methods:

Output:

Layout Design:

Notes

Notes

Pseudocode:	Functions/Views:
	Methods:

Output:

Layout Design:

Notes

Notes

Pseudocode:	Functions/Views:
	Methods:

Output:

Layout Design:

Notes

Notes

Pseudocode:	Functions/Views:
	Methods:

Output:

Layout Design:

Notes

Notes

Pseudocode:	Functions/Views:
	Methods:
Output:	

Layout Design:

Notes

Notes

Pseudocode:	Functions/Views:
	Methods:

Output:

Layout Design:

Notes

Notes

Pseudocode:	Functions/Views:
	Methods:
Output:	

Layout Design:

Notes

Notes

Pseudocode:	Functions/Views:
	Methods:

Output:

Layout Design:

Notes

Notes

Pseudocode:	Functions/Views:
	Methods:

Output:

Layout Design:

Notes

Notes

Pseudocode:	Functions/Views:
	Methods:

Output:

Layout Design:

Notes

Notes

Pseudocode:	Functions/Views:
	Methods:

Output:

Layout Design:

Notes

Notes

Pseudocode:	Functions/Views:
	Methods:

Output:

Layout Design:

Notes

Notes

Pseudocode:	Functions/Views:
	Methods:

Output:

Layout Design:

Notes

Notes

Pseudocode:

Functions/Views:

Methods:

Output:

Layout Design:

Notes

Notes

Pseudocode:	Functions/Views:
	Methods:

Output:

Layout Design:

Notes

Notes

Pseudocode:	Functions/Views:
	Methods:

Output:

Layout Design:

Notes
_____
_____
_____
_____
_____
_____

Notes
_____
_____
_____
_____
_____
_____

Pseudocode:	Functions/Views:
	Methods:

Output:

Layout Design:

Notes

Notes

Pseudocode:	Functions/Views:
	Methods:

Output:

Layout Design:

Notes

Notes

Pseudocode:	Functions/Views:
	Methods:

Output:

Layout Design:

Notes

Notes

Pseudocode:

Functions/Views:

Methods:

Output:

Layout Design:

Notes

Notes

Pseudocode:	Functions/Views:
	Methods:

Output:

Layout Design:

Notes

Notes

Pseudocode:	Functions/Views:
	Methods:
Output:	

Layout Design:

Notes

Notes

Pseudocode:	Functions/Views:
	Methods:

Output:

Layout Design:

Notes

Notes

Pseudocode:	Functions/Views:
	Methods:

Output:

Layout Design:

Notes

Notes

Pseudocode:	Functions/Views:
	Methods:

Output:

Layout Design:

Notes

Notes

Pseudocode:	Functions/Views:
	Methods:

Output:

Layout Design:

Notes

Notes

Pseudocode:	Functions/Views:
	Methods:

Output:

Layout Design:

Notes

Notes

Pseudocode:	Functions/Views:
	Methods:

Output:

Layout Design:

Notes

Notes

Pseudocode:	Functions/Views:
	Methods:
Output:	

Layout Design:

Notes

Notes

Pseudocode:	Functions/Views:
	Methods:

Output:

Layout Design:

Notes

Notes

Pseudocode:	Functions/Views:
	Methods:

Output:

Layout Design:

Notes

Notes

Pseudocode:	Functions/Views:
	Methods:

Output:

Layout Design:

Notes

Notes

Pseudocode:	Functions/Views:
	Methods:

Output:

Layout Design:

Notes

Notes

Pseudocode:	Functions/Views:
	Methods:

Output:

Layout Design:

Notes

Notes

Pseudocode:	Functions/Views:
	Methods:

Output:

Layout Design:

Notes

Notes

Pseudocode:	Functions/Views:
	Methods:

Output:

Layout Design:

Notes

Notes